W9-DJK-214

BK 923.673 R781M
ELEANOR ROOSEVELT STORY
/MACLEISH,
1965 .00 FV
3000 066511 30010
St. Louis Community College

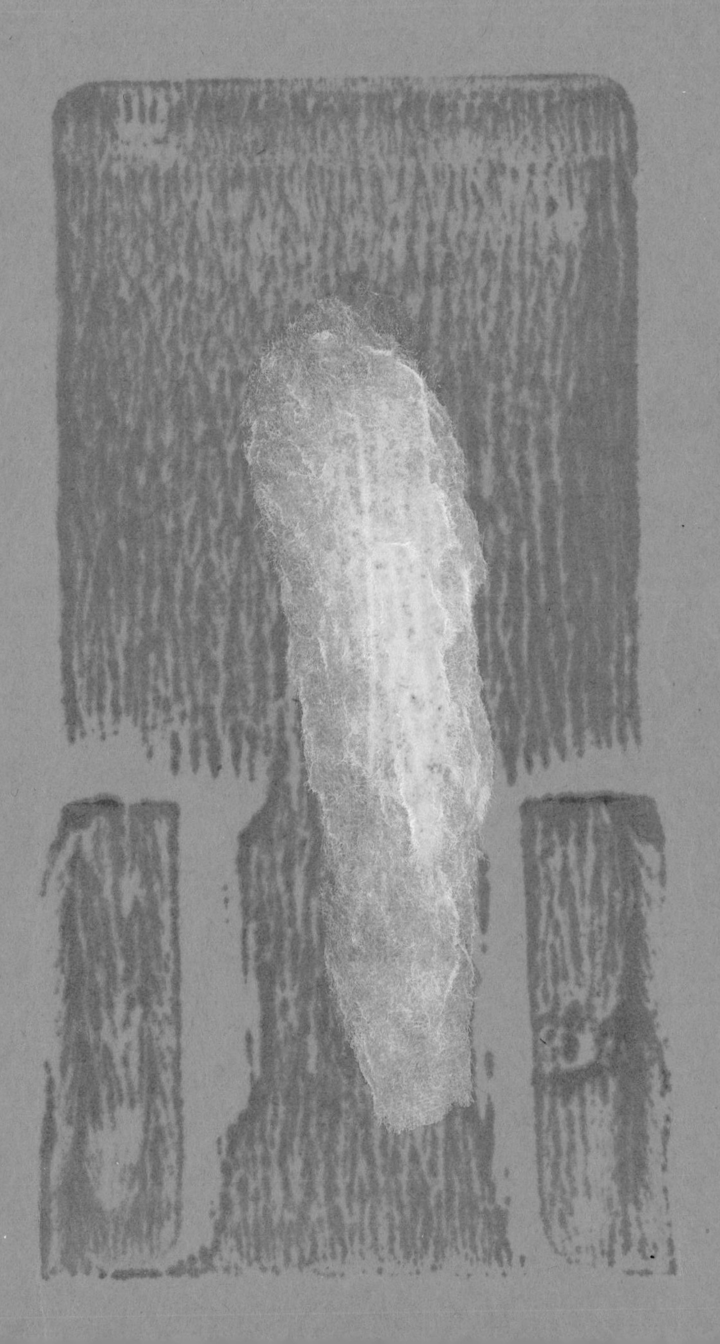

The Eleanor Roosevelt Story

Also by Archibald MacLeish

POEMS

Collected Poems, 1917-1952
including *Conquistador, Streets in the Moon, New Found Land, Act five,* and others
Songs for Eve

PLAYS IN VERSE

Panic
The Fall of the City
Air Raid
The Trojan Horse
This Music Crept by Me upon the Waters
J.B.

PROSE

The Irresponsibles
The American Cause
A Time to Speak
A Time to Act
American Opinion and the War
Poetry and Opinion
Freedom Is the Right to Choose
Poetry and Experience

The Eleanor Roosevelt Story

Archibald MacLeish

HOUGHTON MIFFLIN COMPANY BOSTON

SECOND PRINTING R

Library of Congress Catalog Card Number: 65-26267

Printed in the United States of America

The text and illustrations in this book are from the motion picture The Eleanor Roosevelt Story, *produced by Mr. Sidney Glazier. Portions of the book first appeared in* McCall's *magazine.*

WHERE IS THE dramatic light and shadow in Eleanor Roosevelt's life? Clearly in the contrast — the extraordinary disparity between beginning and end. She dies the object of the world's attention and is buried not only with the ceremonies reserved for the great but with something the greatest rarely achieve — the real grief of millions of human beings. But she was born at the farthest possible remove from all this. Not in poverty and insignificance, but in an almost inexpressible banality. Nothing in history has been more banal than the provinciality of the lives of the rich and well born in the New York of Eleanor Roosevelt's girlhood. Eleanor Roosevelt had no desire as a young girl but to belong to that world. She suffered because she was not the "beauty" her mother's family was supposed to produce, or because she lacked the graces young girls of her class were supposed to have, or because her grandmother, when her grandmother took over her life, didn't approve of her. She was, in short, not only a child of her class and place and time, but a child of her class and place and time who asked for nothing better than to win its approval — and who failed.

And out of *that* comes *this.* Out of a rejected child in the most provincial city of a provincial age comes the most remarkable woman to appear in the twentieth century!

How? My own notion is that the answer might be found in the myth of the sleeping beauty. People aren't "made" by themselves or by anyone else: they are *released to be* what they always were but had never known they were — and what releases them is the touch of life. For thirty years of her life, the woman who was to change the world lay in a sound if not too comfortable sleep back of the thorns and thickets of the decaying castle of the dying age into which she was born. The time came, probably during that most terrible of wars (for the first war was more unbearable than the second, atom bombs or no atom bombs), when the realization came through to her — the burning sense of need, of human suffering — which is to say, of life. And the rest of her history was the playing out of that tremendous discovery.

ARCHIBALD MACLEISH
From a letter to the producer of the film The Eleanor Roosevelt Story

The Eleanor Roosevelt Story

IN THE Rose Garden at Hyde Park beside the grave of her husband, the thirty-second President of the United States, Eleanor Roosevelt is buried. She was seventy-eight years old.

Mrs. Roosevelt's children are there . . . James, Elliott, John, Anna, Franklin Jr.

The President is there — the Presidents: Kennedy with Mrs. Kennedy, Lyndon Johnson, then Vice President; Truman; Eisenhower; Ambassador Adlai Stevenson. It was not her life, as her friend Adlai Stevenson put it, that the world had lost — "She had lived that out to the full. What we have lost," he said, "what we have to recall for ourselves — to remember — is what she was herself: And who can name it?"

Who can name it?

Family Register.

Births.

Anna Eleanor Roosevelt.

October 11th 1884 11 a.m.

God Father. Theodore Roosevelt } lbs. 8½

God Mothers - Mrs Hy Parish Jr { By Dr Hy. Y. Satterlee
Miss E. L. Hall

Elliott Roosevelt Jr

September 29th/89 3 P.M.
12 lbs

God Fathers. James K Gracie } March 10/90
V. G. Hall 56 W 37 -
God-Mother Miss Anna Roosevelt } 5 P.m.
by
Dr Hy. Y. Satterlee

There are fairy tales in all the tongues of the world about children who live under the spell of sleep in a magic prison surrounded by thickets and thorns: a prison from which they are one day awakened by a touch, to turn into shining figures of life. No one knows how they become what they are at the end — only that they are.

What Eleanor Roosevelt remembered, looking back, was an unhappy little girl in a lost family in a vanished world — a child she never could have been, but was!

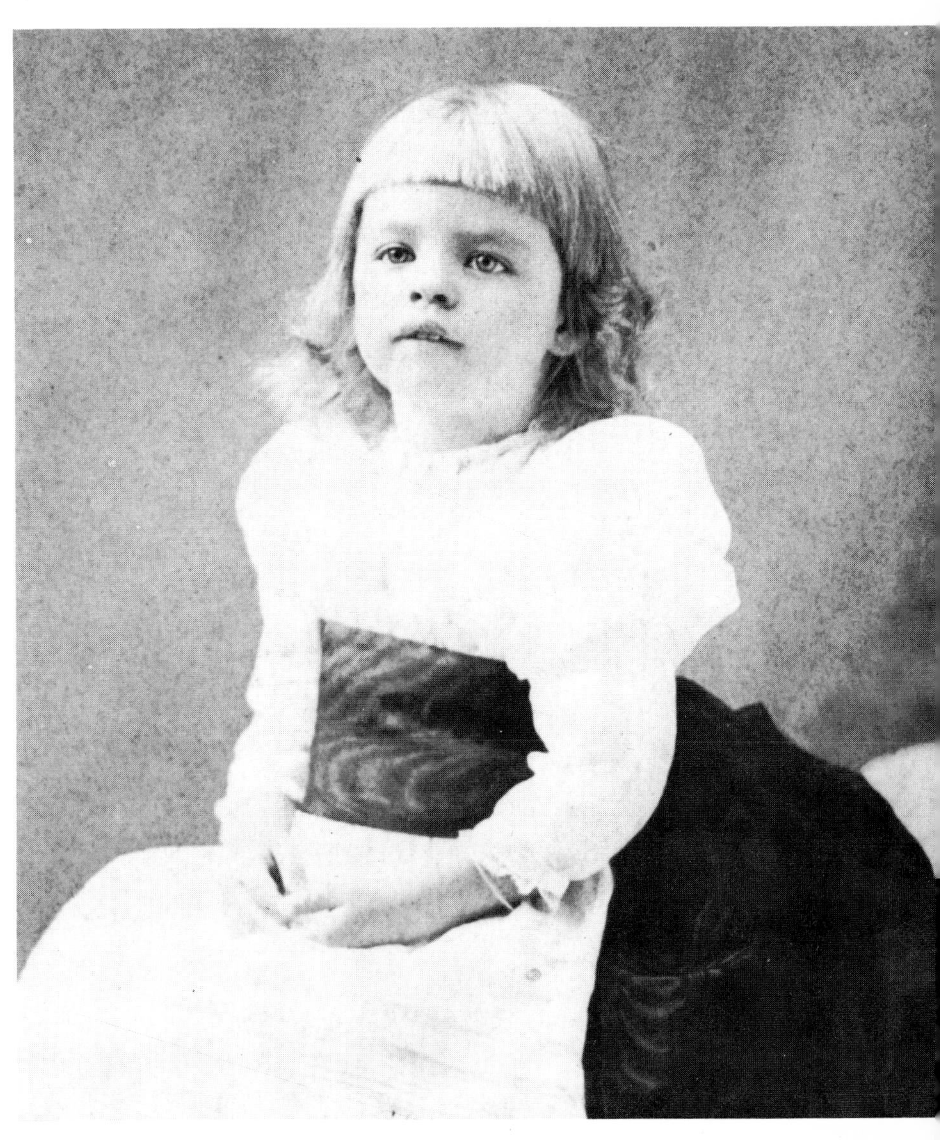

She said that her mother was always a little troubled by her lack of beauty and that she knew it as a child senses those things — and that her pretty young aunts, her mother's sisters, told her so — in so many words.

MRS. ROOSEVELT: One of the aunts was to say to me, "You are the ugly duckling of the family." It was an unknown thing for a Hall girl not to be a belle at every party.

MRS. COLE *(A niece of Theodore Roosevelt and Eleanor Roosevelt's cousin and bridesmaid, the former Corinne Robinson married Joseph Alsop and after his death Francis Cole of Hartford, Connecticut)*: And it was, too. They were a pretty lot — her aunts and her mother . . . above all her mother, whose clothes she loved to stroke. But her mother preferred her little brothers and showed it,

and called her "Granny" because Eleanor was so old-fashioned.

With her father, however, things were different. He called her little Nell and she adored him.

But her relationship with her father was brief. He began drinking when she was quite small and eventually he was sent off to a little town in Virginia. Eleanor never knew why — only that she loved him and he was gone.

A LETTER TO ELEANOR FROM HER FATHER: My darling little Nell . . . Because father is not with you is not because he doesn't love you. For I love you tenderly and dearly — and maybe soon I'll come back well and strong and we will have such good times together, like we used to have.

MRS. COLE: When she was eight her mother died almost overnight: diphtheria went very fast in those days.

And her brother, Elliott, also died of diphtheria. And Eleanor and her baby brother went to live with her Grandmother Hall on Thirty-seventh Street and, in the summers, at Tivoli on the Hudson.

I remember the Thirty-seventh Street home as the darkest, most desolate house I have ever seen.

And Tivoli, too, was grim and lonely.

MRS. ROOSEVELT: I was six years older than my brother, and so in the country there were no children my age at all and we went there for practically five months every year.

MRS. COLE: There were no children her age to play with and later, when her Uncle Vallie began drinking, none were allowed — no one who did not know the family well enough to "understand."

One day Eleanor said to my mother, "Auntie, I have no real home," and burst into tears.

And then, when she was not quite ten, her father died as the result of a riding accident and she was really alone.

Alone with her Grandmother Hall who had been a Miss Ludlow and a great belle in her youth, and who lived all her life as though the entire world were "society."

MRS. ROOSEVELT: To my family this society was all important. There didn't exist anything that was as important as this small, closed-in society, largely at that time presided over by Mrs. Astor and looked upon, by those who really thought it important, as practically the only people who existed.

MRS. COLE: Eleanor belonged to that world of course, and she knew its customs.

But though she "belonged" she was never a part of it: her sadness and loneliness set her apart.

And yet, for the rest of us, it was a lovely world to be young in — to go dancing in — to do all the things that seemed simpler and surer and pleasanter than they ever could have been, we thought, in any other time or place.

MRS. ROOSEVELT: My grandmother was convinced that the world she was brought up in was the world that was always going to exist . . . it was never suggested to me that the world was going to be different.

MRS. COLE: Not that that world of ours was merely a pleasant world.

Eleanor's and my grandfather, Theodore Roosevelt's father, had founded the Newsboys Club, now called the Children's Aid Society, and when we were quite small we used to be taken to help serve Christmas Dinner.

MRS. ROOSEVELT: I had this horrible sense of obligation which was bred in me. I couldn't help it.

MRS. COLE: Her "horrible sense of obligation" and a deep and isolating sense of loneliness — of life in a dream — made life difficult for Eleanor.

After her father's death Eleanor was seldom allowed to visit her Roosevelt relatives . . . and when we did see her at Uncle Ted's she felt at a great disadvantage because she was not used to companions her own age.

And her education, too, had been neglected. When she was six her Great-aunt Ludlow discovered to her horror that Eleanor couldn't read.

Mrs. Roosevelt: I had learned French before I learned English, from a French nurse who was bad for my character but good for my language.

My grandmother felt that she was doing the best she knew how. She was sending me to the most fashionable little class conducted by a pompous old gentleman named Mr. Rosa.

Mrs. Cole: That wasn't the whole of her childhood education, of course.

Finally, when she was fifteen, it was decided to send her to a French school in England which our Auntie Bye had attended when it was at Versailles before the Franco-Prussian War.

Its headmistress, Mlle Souvestre, was a remarkable woman, with strong ideas of her own. She thought that the verdict in the Dreyfus case was outrageous — as, of course, it was — and that the British were to blame in the Boer War, and all this she used to say in the most fearless manner and to the lively interest of all of us.

The years at school with Mlle Souvestre must have been like the opening of a window in Eleanor's life.

When she came back at the end of her three years it was to return to Tivoli where Uncle Vallie was worse and her grandmother almost entirely preoccupied with her fears of what he might do.

Tivoli, that summer, was a grim, closed miserable world of its own — not a very good preparation for being a gay and joyous debutante.

Coming out in New York at the turn of the century was something of an ordeal for anyone: for Eleanor it was a nightmare.

"That first winter," she said, "when my sole object in life was society, nearly brought me to a state of nervous collapse."

She was a stranger in her own world and worse — almost an outcast. "There was absolutely nothing about me," she said, "to attract anybody's attention."

She was wrong, of course, and it was about this time she began seeing something of her cousin Franklin — fifth cousin once removed.

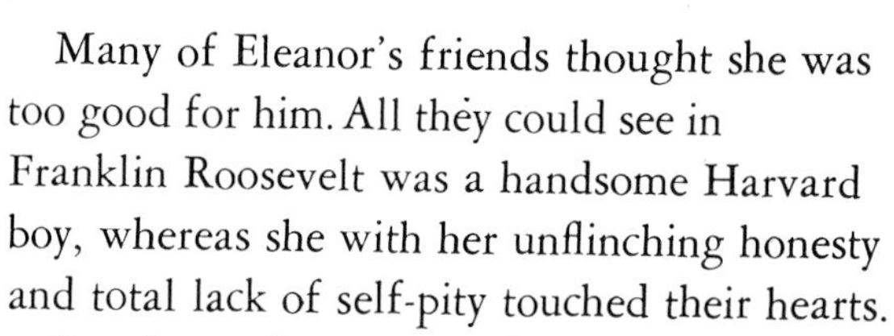

Many of Eleanor's friends thought she was too good for him. All they could see in Franklin Roosevelt was a handsome Harvard boy, whereas she with her unflinching honesty and total lack of self-pity touched their hearts.

But then, of course, he felt the same way. He had somehow the maturity and insight to recognize Eleanor for what she was under all that surface awkwardness and embarrassment.

In the fall of 1903, when she was nineteen and he twenty-one, he asked her to marry him. It seemed, she said, "an entirely natural thing" — the sort of thing you *did.*

But she also said, long afterward, that it was years before she understood "what being in love was or what loving really meant."

As for Franklin, he too had his difficulties; he had his widowed mother, Sara Delano Roosevelt, a formidable and in many ways, a remarkable woman.

A LETTER FROM FRANKLIN DELANO ROOSEVELT TO HIS MOTHER: Dearest Mama, I know what pain I must have caused you and you know I wouldn't do it if I really could have helped it . . . you know that nothing can ever change what we have always been and always will be to each other — only now you have two children to love and to love you — and Eleanor as you know will always be a daughter to you in every true way. Your ever loving F.D.R.

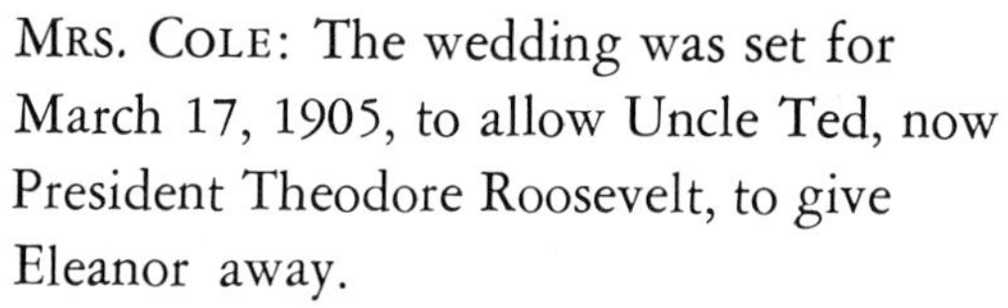

Mrs. Cole: The wedding was set for March 17, 1905, to allow Uncle Ted, now President Theodore Roosevelt, to give Eleanor away.

Franklin and Eleanor were married in the Ludlow house at 8 East Seventy-fifth Street by the Reverend Endicott Peabody. It was a most exciting affair with the bridesmaids — I was one — in cream taffeta.

But when the reception began, the bride and groom found themselves deserted. Uncle Ted had gone into the Library where the refreshments were and the wedding guests had followed the President in a body. Finally Eleanor and Franklin followed, too.

Eleanor thought of herself in those years as a curious mixture of extreme innocence and unworldliness with a great deal of knowledge of some of the less attractive and less agreeable sides of life.

"I had painfully high ideals," she said, "and a tremendous sense of duty, entirely unrelieved by any sense of humor or any appreciation of the weaknesses of human nature."

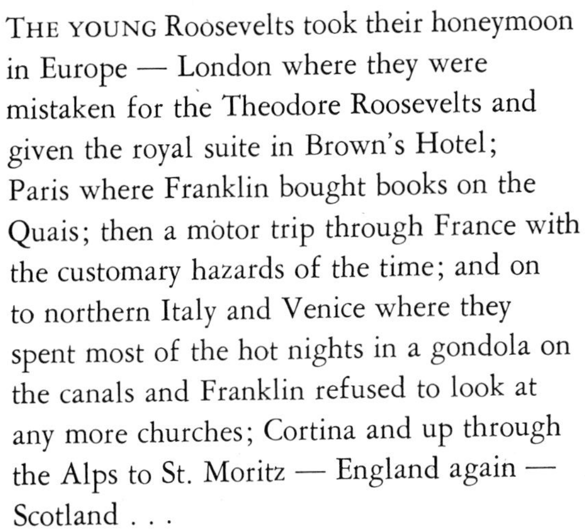

THE YOUNG Roosevelts took their honeymoon in Europe — London where they were mistaken for the Theodore Roosevelts and given the royal suite in Brown's Hotel; Paris where Franklin bought books on the Quais; then a motor trip through France with the customary hazards of the time; and on to northern Italy and Venice where they spent most of the hot nights in a gondola on the canals and Franklin refused to look at any more churches; Cortina and up through the Alps to St. Moritz — England again — Scotland . . .

And so home — to a little house on East Thirty-sixth Street three blocks from Franklin's mother's house, which she had rented for them and furnished and provided with servants.

Eleanor was beginning, she said, to be an "entirely dependent person," driving with her mother-in-law every afternoon, taking at least one meal with her every day, and generally doing whatever she was told.

It was a pleasant enough time in her life. Some of the shyness wore off. She began, as she put it, "to fit into this pattern of a fairly conventional, quiet, young, society matron."

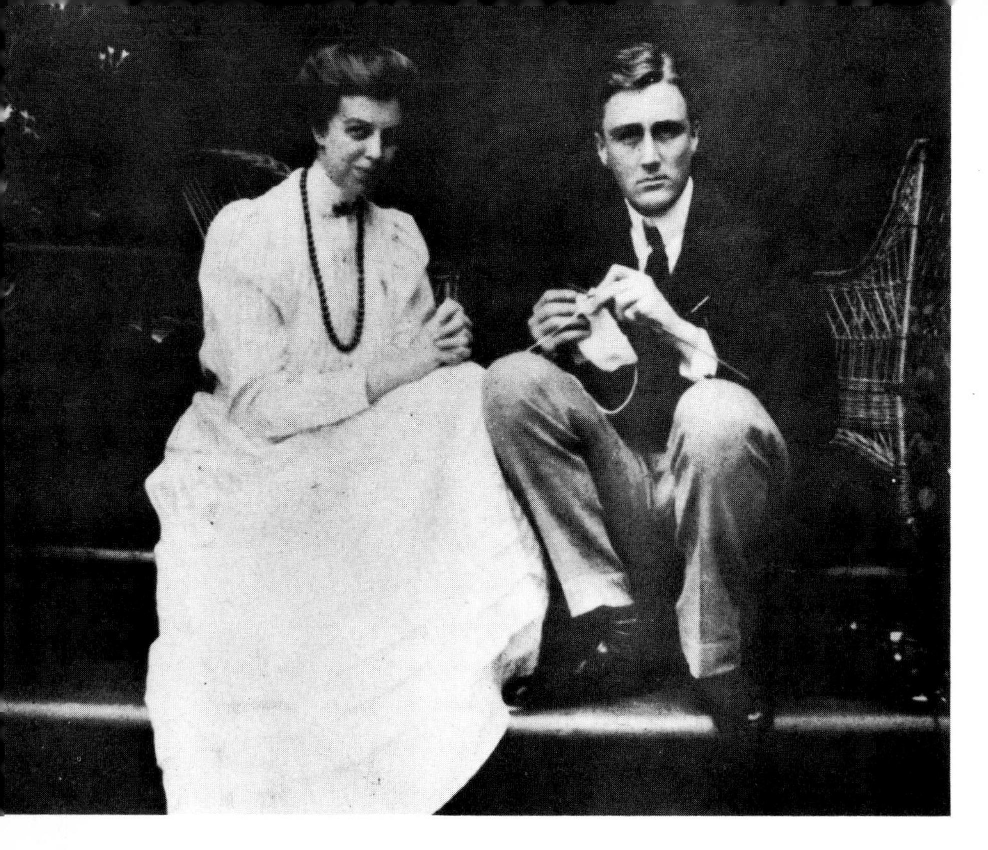

That was the pattern she continued to fit into for the next ten years and more. She was a dutiful wife, a docile daughter-in-law, and a constant mother, bearing child after child,

living in houses her mother-in-law owned or built or rented, in cities her husband's law practice or political activities or government service took him to — New York, Albany, Washington.

When Franklin became Assistant Secretary of the Navy in Woodrow Wilson's Cabinet in 1913, she accepted what she called the slavery of the Washington social system without question. *Her* job, Eleanor insisted, was "to do exactly as the majority of women were doing — perhaps to be a little more meticulous about it." And she was.

If the story of Eleanor Roosevelt had ended in 1917, there would have been little enough to remember: a lonely and dutiful little girl, a self-effacing young wife, a frequent mother, a conventional woman of her place and time, who nevertheless was not a part of her place and time . . . a shy and lonely ghost wandering under the trees of a Hyde Park she could never think of, she said, as home.

But the story did not end in 1917 . . . it began then.

By 1917 that world of Eleanor's grandmother, that world that "was always going to exist," had stopped existing — stopped in a welter of meaningless and idiotic death and destruction in the old Europe out of which it had come.

The hidden flaw in the structure of modern history was cracking open in one country after another around the world and nothing would ever be the same again.

Men died — millions of them — who had barely begun to live. And men began to live — and women too — who had had no lives before. Eleanor Roosevelt was one.

MRS. ROOSEVELT: I went into the canteen which served in the railroad yard, and I suddenly began to understand what some of the conditions were in our country. We were sending men to fight who had no idea where they were going or why.

SHE WAS face to face with something she had never guessed or dared to guess before.

Not the realization that the world outside was a tragic world; she had always known that — she had learned that by suffering herself. Rather the sudden perception that there was something *she* could do about it — she herself — Eleanor Roosevelt, dutiful and obedient child, and girl and woman.

One can almost name the day of that realization. She had driven over to Saint Elizabeth's, the Federal Insane Asylum, where her husband's department, the Navy, had taken over a block of buildings for shell-shocked sailors and marines.

What she saw as she drove through the the grounds horrified her: "Poor demented creatures," she said, "with apparently very little attention being paid them, gazing from behind bars or walking up and down on enclosed porches."

REPORT HORRORS AT ST. ELIZABETH'S

Officials Tell Committee on Appropriations of Needs of Twenty-Five Hundred Insane Soldiers.

BY N. O. MESSENGER.

WITHIN sight of the Capitol building, almost in the shadow of the dome if the sun set in that direction, lies St. Elizabeth's Hospital, the domicile of 2,500 insane soldiers and sailors, together with 1,600 residents of the District of Columbia, which must be an institution of ghastly horrors, according to the reports of officials made to the House committee on appropriations. How congressmen can read the testimony of these officials, which is to be found in the printed hearings on the sundry civil appropriation bill, beginning at page 188, and available to any one, and not be moved to pity and resolve to go the limit :

"If you can give trained attention, you can save many of these men. Fifty per cent of them can be saved. The condition at present

NEED MORE CARE THAN INFANTS.

is pitiable. For instance, with 600 bed-ridden paralytics and patients of that kind, there are not enough people to take care of them. These bed-ridden, helpless ones must lie for hours in a distressed condition because they can not be decently attended to.

"It is our particular desire," said Admiral Braisted, speaking for the management, "not to conceal anything. The complaints have been numerous. The Secretary of the Interior has been swamped with complaints. All the better class of people who are interested in this of work in the city are arou...

The ... had ... and ... lent ... ma... ton ... recki... comm... and a... ture o... to tran... chair" around anothe... promp... ment... mobi... parat...

"Conc... Braisted...

PATIENT... MANY C...

there safel... doctors to ... each case ... ants to ... without ... quately ... have, ... out d... to se... W...

Before the war she would have kept her horror to herself, acquiescing in the world the way it was. Now she acted. She went to the Secretary of the Interior whose department was responsible for Saint Elizabeth's, told him he "had better go over and see" for himself; kept after him until he had persuaded the Congress to increase the hospital's appropriations; got a charitable organization to contribute five hundred dollars for occupational therapy; hounded the Red Cross to build a recreation room.

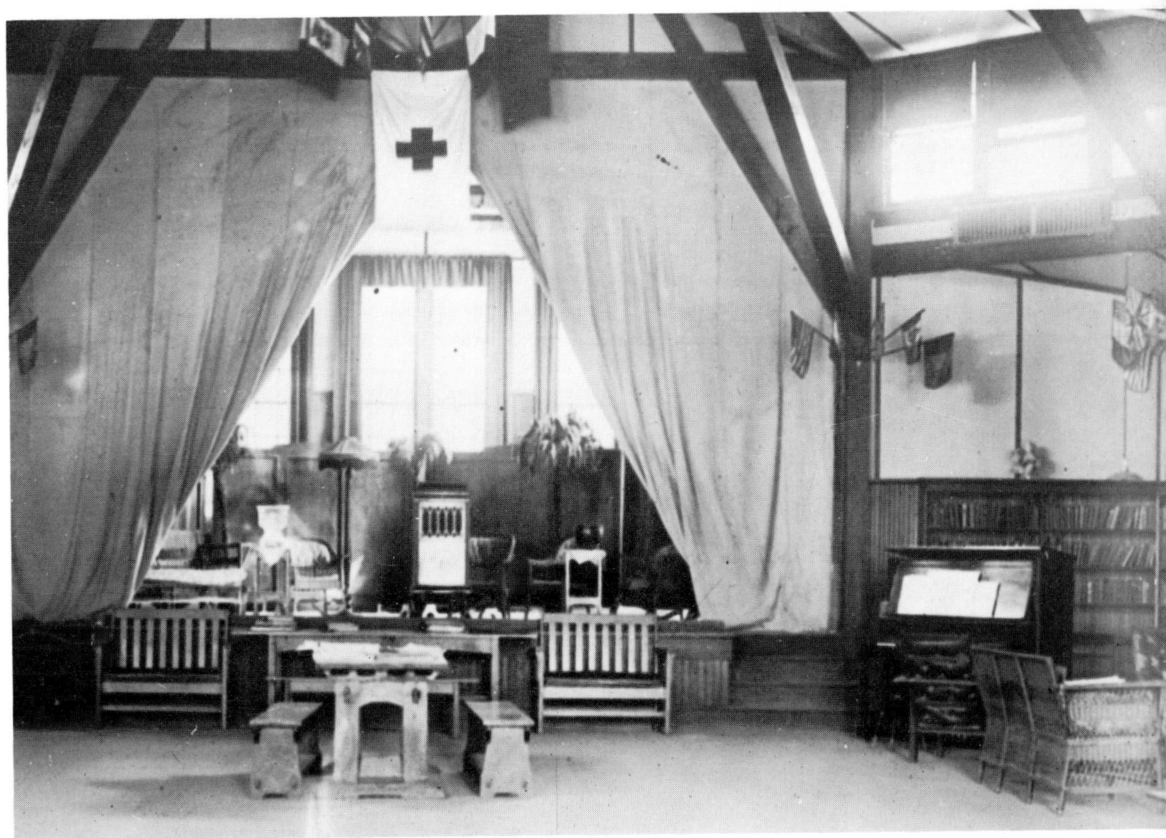

A new force had appeared in the world although the world would not know it for some years to come; a woman who accepted personal responsibility for her country and her time — a citizen who took self-government personally and seriously and would not rest until she had done what she felt she had to do.

She had learned a lesson — a lesson she put for herself in nine words: "What one has to do usually can be done . . ." meaning that what her conscience demanded of her she would henceforth somehow accomplish.

There was another lesson that went with it: Hope is not enough.

In the fall of 1918, the "Great War," "The World War," ended in the brightest moment of hope in modern times — the hope for an end of war, for a parliament of mankind, a League of Nations.

It was a hope that came out of America in the proposal of an American President, and the people of Europe went mad with joy.

Eleanor Roosevelt, who was in Europe with her husband, was a witness of that hope. Returning home on the same ship as

Woodrow Wilson she was also a witness to his campaign across the United States on behalf of the League, and to the maneuvers of the enemies of the League of Nations, headed by Senator Henry Cabot Lodge — and to the final tragedy: the death of the hope — and the death of a man.

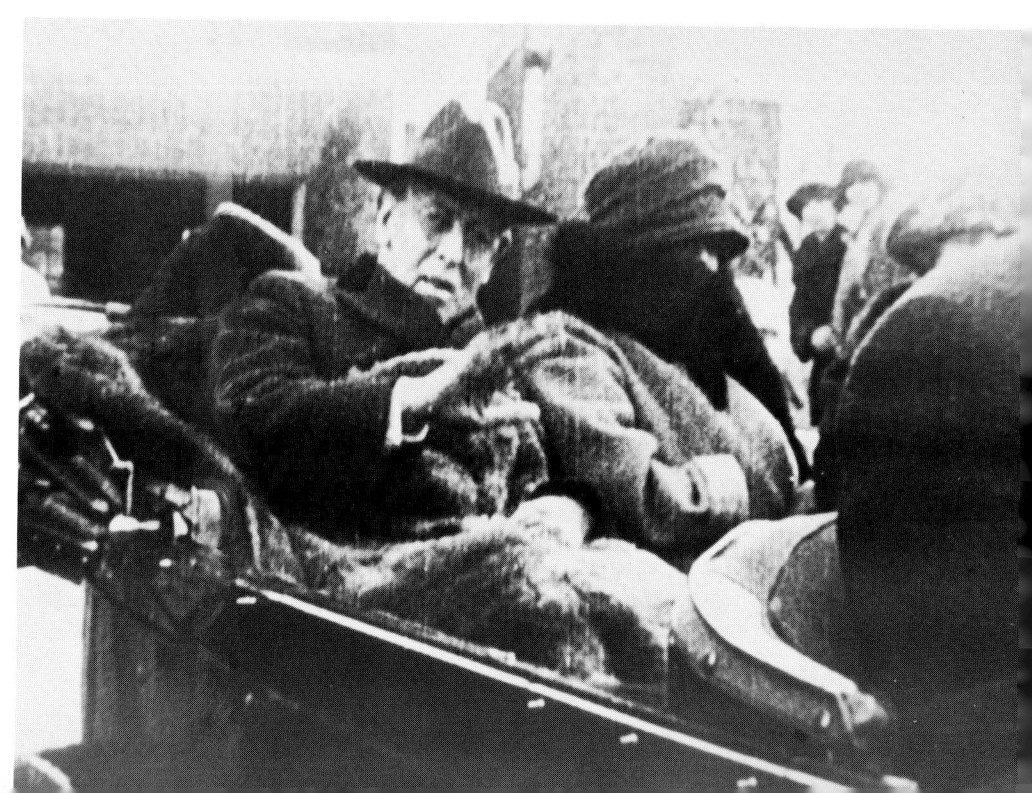

Nothing was left of all that suffering and aspiration but the grave of the Unknown Soldier in Arlington Cemetery — that, and the graves of all the others around the world.

America returned to what Warren Harding, the Republican candidate for the presidency in 1920, called "normalcy," and Eleanor watched it go. Her husband was the Democratic candidate for the Vice Presidency and she saw the whole campaign, beginning with Franklin's notification at Hyde Park. She watched her husband and his running mate James Cox through the long weeks of train trips and speeches and parades . . . until their final defeat in November.

"Normalcy" for the young Roosevelts meant a return to domesticity, to the practice of the law and to what Eleanor called a winter "with nothing but teas, luncheons and dinners to take up time" — "an impossible mode of living" after the realities of the war.

Eleanor Roosevelt and her husband were caught with the rest of that generation in a dead eddy of time like the suck of a bathtub running out — the circling, directionless eddy we call "the Twenties" — a time when time existed to be spent — lost — forgotten.

Except that Eleanor Roosevelt never wasted anything — least of all time. She learned to write shorthand, to cook, to type. And a winter passed and a spring . . . and suddenly for Eleanor Roosevelt and her husband, even that meaningless clock stopped.

One day he was sailing his boat at Campobello, swimming in the Bay of Fundy — a tall man, handsome, vigorous as all the Roosevelts were vigorous

. . . and the next he was a helpless cripple — paralyzed, his legs useless. He was not yet forty and he would never move again without awkwardness and difficulty and pain.

His life, his political, public life was over. His mother knew that: he would return to Hyde Park as the invalid he was and live there.

But there was one man who didn't know it — Louis Howe, the little newspaperman from Albany.

And there was a woman who didn't know it either: Eleanor, his wife.

Why? You can answer for Louis Howe. He was a superb politician, a kingmaker, and he knew a king when he saw one. You can answer for Louis Howe, but why did Eleanor Roosevelt agree with him? Fight her mother-in-law for her husband's soul? Struggle through "the most trying winter," as she called it, of her entire life.

She knew it was kinder, gentler, to that suffering and uncomplaining husband of hers to let him be, as his mother wanted to let him be, as most wives would have wanted to let him be.

She knew that pain and disappointment and public humiliation might well lie ahead. And yet she persisted, staked her womanhood on it, her husband's affection, her mother-in-law's goodwill, her family's happiness.

Why? Because she had learned that "what one has to do usually can be done"? Because she felt there was something her husband *had to do?*

All we know for certain is that she won her fight.

Eleanor Roosevelt entered politics herself first through the Women's Trade Union League and then as a member of the Women's Division of the Democratic State Committee to draw her husband's interest back to the political world.

By 1924 Franklin Roosevelt had made the difficult return. At the Democratic National Convention he nominated Al Smith for the presidency, likening him to "the Happy Warrior." But to those who listened, the Happy Warrior was the broken man with the confident, smiling face who stood there balanced precariously on his crutches, taking up his life again.

The great gamble had paid off. Franklin Roosevelt was back in the world again — so firmly back that four years later the State Convention of his Party nominated him for the governorship of New York — back so effectively that when the Democratic national ticket lost New York in 1928, he carried it.

The two Roosevelts, Franklin and Eleanor, had the future in their hands.

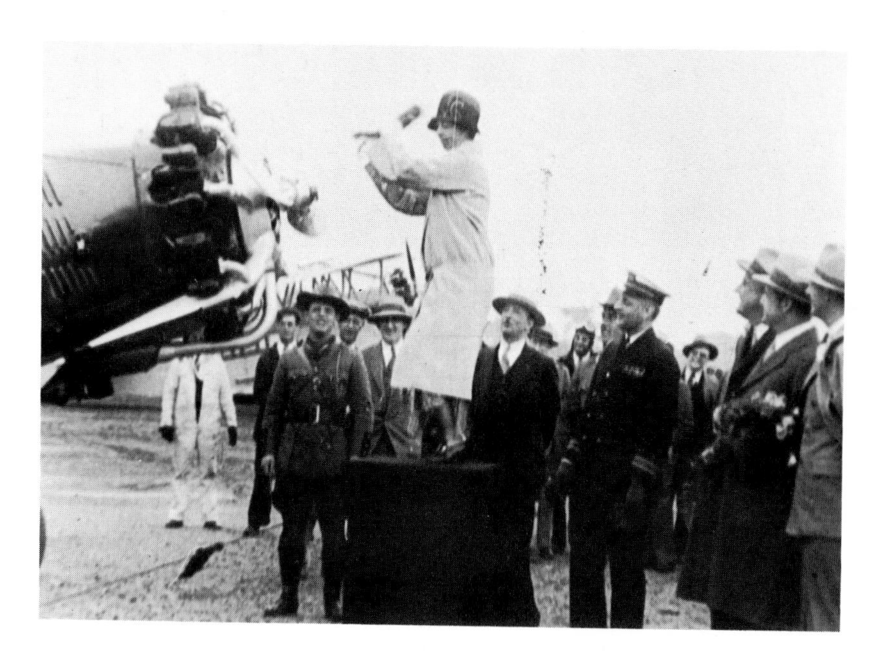

Looking around her from that triumphant moment Eleanor Roosevelt could see, what before she could only have guessed. There was indeed something "to be done."

Hitler was on the rise in Germany.

Corruption in the Harding Cabinet had shaken the faith of Americans in their government.

And the eight years of stockmarket profits that had paid for the dizzy dance of the twenties were about at an end. The market crashed, and the world came crumbling down into the Great Depression that the war had dug for it — the pit at the world's end — or at the end, at least, of *one* world.

Breadlines appeared in every city. Self-respecting men with shame in their faces sold pencils and apples in the streets and their children went hungry.

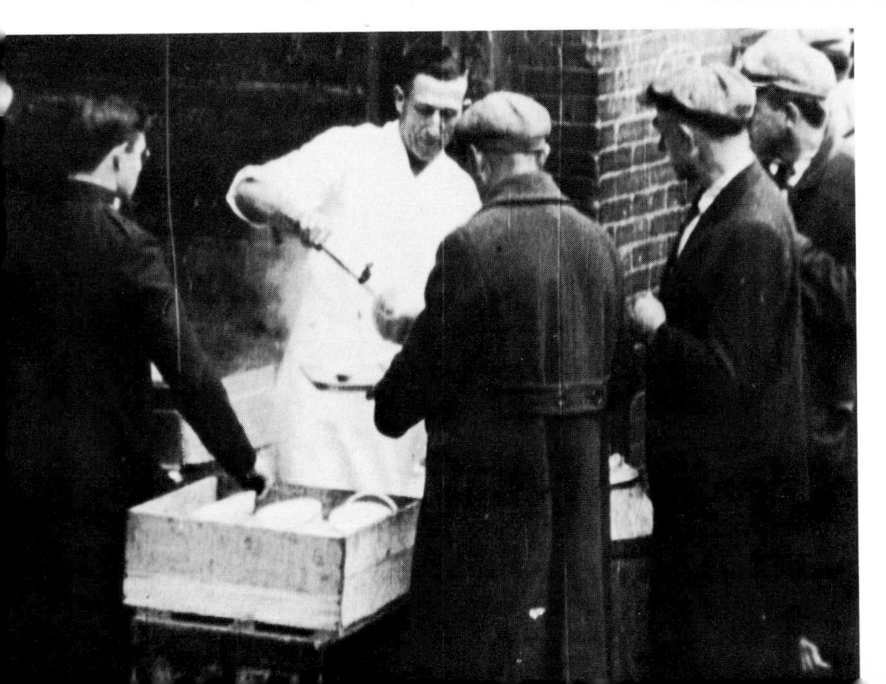

Eleanor Roosevelt reacted as she always had to human suffering — personally. She gave her card to the miserable in Times Square, invited the hungry to her own table.

But it wasn't that kind of misery.

Before Hoover's term was out, veterans of the World War marched on Washington to demand the immediate payment of a bonus.

They were met by Smedley Butler, a famous general of Marines.

BUTLER: It's an honor — a privilege to come here and be with you. I mean just what I say. I don't want anything. Nobody can kick me anymore. I'll say what I think. You have just as much right to have a lobby here as any steel corporation. First, don't make any mistake about it, you've got the sympathy of the American people. Now don't you lose it. We've got a God-given form of government and whether it's run right or not depends on the people who do the voting.

BUT WORDS — even the homely words of General Butler — were no answer to a hungry stomach. Eventually the Bonus Marchers, as they were called, were driven out of Washington by General MacArthur acting under President Hoovers's orders.

By now it was obvious to others than Eleanor Roosevelt that there were things to be done.

Only what?

And by whom?

The election of 1932 answered the second half of that question. A tall man, his legs braced in a metal contraption, his face confident among frightened faces, arrived at the White House in March of 1933. He drove up Pennsylvania Avenue with the outgoing President, Herbert Hoover, beside him. Took the oath of office on the Capitol steps and said:

F.D.R: . . . first of all let me assert my firm belief that the only thing we have to fear is fear itself.

Our greatest primary task is to put people to work. This is pre-eminently the time to speak the truth, the whole truth frankly and boldly. Nor need we shrink from honestly facing conditions in our country today. This nation is asking for action, and action now.

BUT WHAT type of action? The first half of the question remained: *What* should be done? What *could* be done? The wreckage in the great Republic was *human* wreckage. *People* had been hurt, frightened, bewildered. How did you deal with *people?*

The new economists in the White House had their theories: Eleanor Roosevelt had hers.

Only hers were never theories, but actions. On the 15th of May she drove down to the Anacostia flats in her own car to talk to a new group of Bonus Marchers.

And that year, as the Depression deepened and the winter came on, she began to speak her own mind in her own way.

MRS. ROOSEVELT: The needs are going to be great this coming winter. There will be, I hope, more people employed, but those who are not employed will need more than they have needed before. Their clothes have completely gone, their courage is not as high as it was a year ago. So there is no reason for letting up in our sense of responsibility.

CERTAINLY *she* never let up: she went everywhere misery was to be found — and that was everywhere in those days — everywhere misery could be found and everywhere misery could be fought . . .

Up in the air on the sling of one of the great cranes building dams for the Tennessee Valley Authority . . .

Down to earth in one of the rural slums where the Resettlement Administration was building hospitals . . . teaching skills . . . feeding children . . . *Underground* in West Virginia or Pennsylvania or Illinois where the mines were dying, and men were out of work, and the equipment was idle.

Until she became an American legend of ubiquity, of ceaseless movement — running . . . flying . . . dancing; an American myth of measureless energy, an inexhaustible theme for wisecracks . . . some of them, like Jack Benny's, kind . . .

MRS. ROOSEVELT: I am very happy to buy this ticket from you, Mr. Benny. How much do I owe you?
JACK BENNY: Well, that's twenty-five cents, for one ticket.
MRS. ROOSEVELT: Can you give me change for a dollar?
JACK BENNY: Well, I haven't the change with me just now, but I'll be glad to send it to you . . . if you'll just stay in one place.

Until she became, was, something more —
a center of controversy, the kind of
controversy that conscience in action —
personal conscience in personal action —
always provokes.

CONGRESSMAN RANDOLPH *(Chairman of Congressional Committee)*: Mrs. Roosevelt, you are the first First Lady of the land who has appeared before a Congressional Committee. I can assure you that we are deeply appreciative of your presence.

Mrs. Roosevelt, would you please tell the Committee about the conditions as you found them on your visits to the various welfare institutions.

MRS. ROOSEVELT: I came away with the feeling that if in the United States, Blue Plains was our conception of how to care for the aged we were at a pretty low ebb of civilization. It was a sick feeling you got from the whole atmosphere.

HER OWN KIND — her own class, as they called themselves — found it difficult to forgive talk as honest as that: anyone who saw unpleasant things and mentioned them was palpably an enemy of the established order.

And journalists of a certain stripe agreed, with the result that the President's wife became the target of column after column of almost daily vituperation.

Some patriotic organizations disapproved and one, the Daughters of the American Revolution, expressed its dissent from her well-known views on racial discrimination by refusing the use of its Washington auditorium to one of the finest of American singers because she sang in a dark skin.

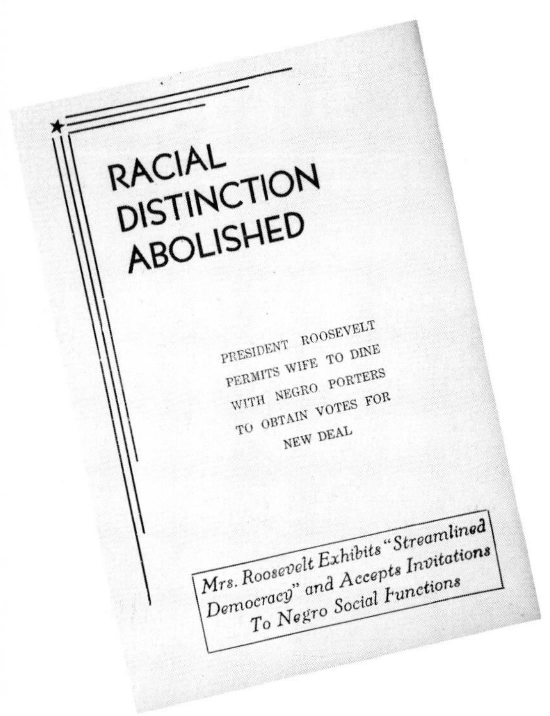
RACIAL DISTINCTION ABOLISHED

PRESIDENT ROOSEVELT PERMITS WIFE TO DINE WITH NEGRO PORTERS TO OBTAIN VOTES FOR NEW DEAL

Mrs. Roosevelt Exhibits "Streamlined Democracy" and Accepts Invitations To Negro Social Functions

Marion Anderson, needless to say, was not embarrassed by the refusal: she appeared instead at the Lincoln Memorial as a guest of the government of the United States.

And Eleanor Roosevelt was not embarrassed: she had more Revolutionary soldiers in her ancestry than many of her fellow members put together and needed the Daughters far less than the Daughters needed her.

But the President *was* concerned as the abuse became uglier, and eventually he put his wife's detractors in their proper places.

F.D.R.: These Republican leaders have not been content with attacks on me or on my wife or on my son.

No . . . not content with that, they now include my little dog Fala. Well, of course *I* don't resent attacks and my *family* don't resent attacks . . . but *Fala* does resent them . . .

MRS. ROOSEVELT: You know, curiously enough, I never minded criticism much. I think I learned very young to know that everything passes and if you just live it through it comes to an end. If there is criticism and there is a foundation of right in it, well then it's their criticism and you have to take it. If there is no foundation in it, sooner or later people are going to find it out and in the meantime, it doesn't really matter much.

The only thing I would mind would be if it really affected the people I loved — people whose feeling of affection it really disturbed.

AND OF COURSE it never did affect the people she loved.

People were everything to her; not only her own people but all the others everywhere. And it is largely for this reason that her understanding of her own time — of the tragic and violent events that made up her own time — seems sounder in retrospect

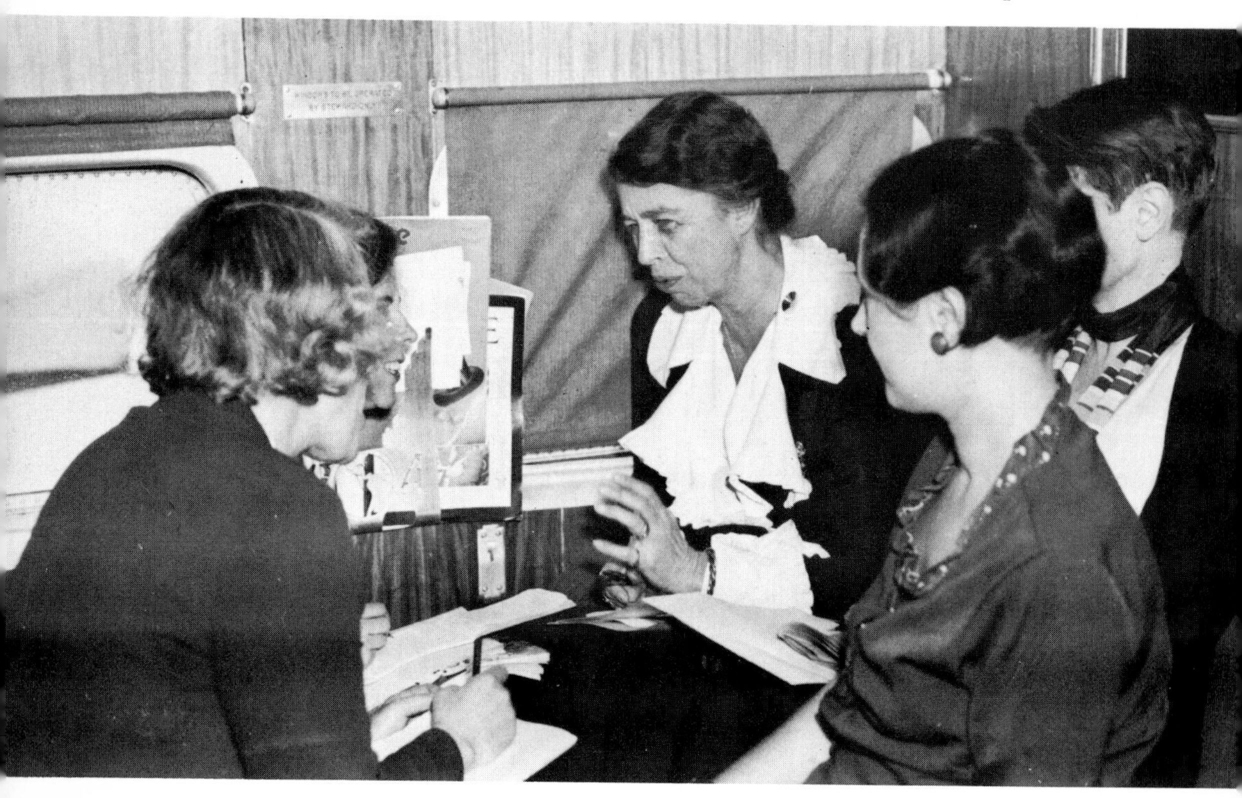

than the understanding of many of her
husband's best-informed advisers. They
thought in terms of policies; she thought in
terms of people. Hitler to her was not a new
political leader who might or might not
change the balance of power in Europe: he
was a perverter of humanity — including the
humanity of the German people and

particularly of the German young. Franco was not a general who had checked Russian ambitions in Spain: he was a Fascist who had overthrown the first hopeful Republican government Spain had ever had and turned the country back into a police state from which thousands of Spaniards escaped as best they could.

It is for this reason too that she understood long before the majority of the American people that Fascism and Nazism were dangers not only in Europe but to our own continent and Republic as well.

The real question, she saw, was the human question. The issue everywhere — Russia, Germany, Italy, Spain — was the issue of human decency, human freedom. And the ultimate outcome would depend on human choice — particularly the choice and decision of the young.

Feeling as she did, Eleanor Roosevelt could hardly help expressing her feelings, President's wife or not.

Mrs. Roosevelt: All of us have an equal responsibility in the one great country that is free . . . to the rest of the word wherever there may be people who are not free to become free again . . .

And the dictatorships replied in kind. Goebbels called her a figure of fun, a silly woman talking of things that should be reserved for politicians. Mussolini attacked her as a nuisance who should be embargoed. And Franco added his bitter word from behind the skirts of his defenders. None of this, needless to say, interested Eleanor Roosevelt. She was not concerned with what Nazis and Communists thought of her: only what her fellow countrymen thought of Nazism and Communism. Democracy was on trial even in the United States where voices were already arguing for a change in American purposes toward the left or toward the right.

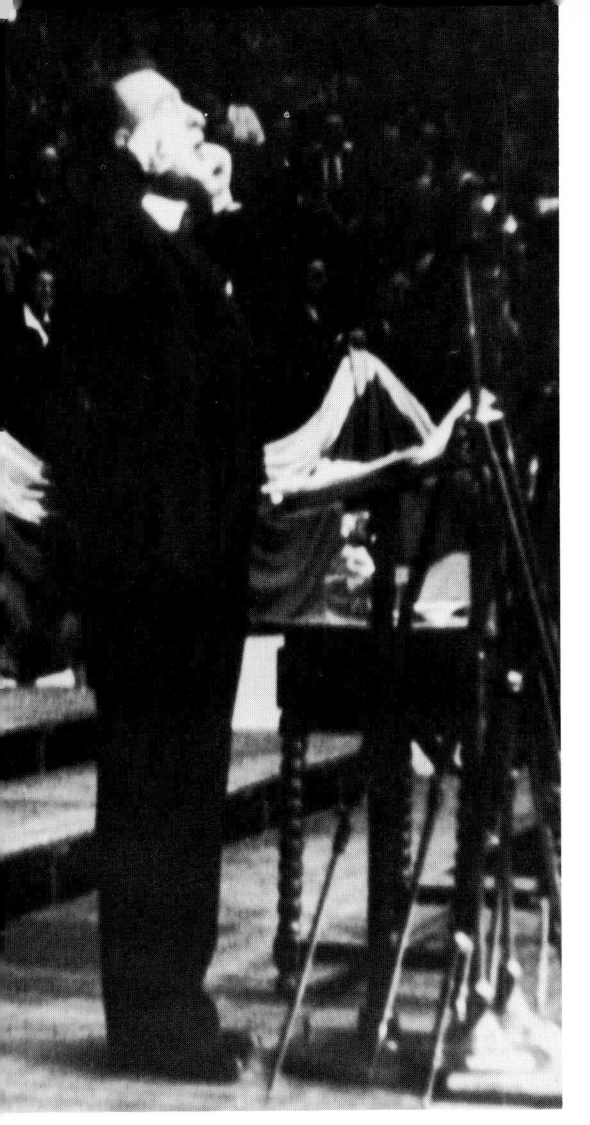

FATHER COUGHLIN: I ask you in the name of Christianity, which abhors Communism, in the name of patriotism which loves America, to carry it on to victory. I ask you if you will rise in your places, and pledge with me to restore America to the Americans.

WHAT MATTERED to Mrs. Roosevelt was not the speakers but the response — above all the response of the young. If young Americans decided, as some already had, that authoritarianism was "the wave of the future," then freedom and self-government in America would also disappear.

The young generation of those years had grown up in the universal disillusionment after the World War.

They believed the generation before them had been "had" by the imperialists of Germany and England and France. They were determined not to be "had" themselves.

They were persuaded, many of them, that the way not to be "had" was to support the Russian Revolution which had rejected the World War in 1917: to become Communists or to follow the Communist Party Line.

Most of their elders in the thirties reacted by denunciations and threats: young Communists were criminals who should be hounded by Congressional Committees such as that headed by Congressman Martin Dies and exposed — excommunicated — if possible deported.

Not so Mrs. Roosevelt. She could understand perfectly well why young people might call themselves Communists in the conditions of the thirties. But she understood also how little chance Communism had to hold the allegiance of the young if the young had a free chance to decide for themselves.

For this reason, and despite considerable criticism, Mrs. Roosevelt had extended her hospitality and her friendship to a number of leftward-looking youth organizations — and even at a time when she herself was under attack in the Communist press.

In the winter of 1939–40, the American Youth Congress, largest and most vocal of these groups, held a meeting in Washington and invited Mrs. Roosevelt to speak.

By that time the issue between the young leftists and American opinion in general was sharply drawn: the Nazi-Soviet Pact had been signed six months earlier, and World War II had already begun with the German invasion of Poland.

When the Soviet Union attacked Finland the sympathy of most Americans, Eleanor Roosevelt included, was with the Finns — while the Youth Congress followed the Russian line in calling Finland the "aggressor."

But despite these differences Mrs. Roosevelt agreed to attend their meeting and answer their questions. Her husband, at her request, had addressed the delegates first, 4500 of them, standing in the rain in the White House garden while the President characterized their views on the Finnish war as "unadulterated twaddle."

F.D.R.: It has been said that some of you are Communists. That is a very unpopular term today. As Americans you have a right, a legal and constitutional right, to call yourselves Communists — those of you who do. You have a right peacefully and openly to advocate certain ideas of theoretical Communism. But as Americans, you have not only a right but a sacred duty to confine your advocacy of changes in law to the methods prescribed by the Constitution of the United States. You have no American right by act or deed to subvert the Constitution of the United States.

BY THE TIME Mrs. Roosevelt's turn finally came, the atmosphere was sullen and hostile. But she gave candid, uncompromising, and courteous answers to loaded and often insulting questions.

MRS. ROOSEVELT: I agree with you in your sympathy for Spain. I agree with you in your sympathy for China and Czechoslovakia; but I also have sympathy for Finland.

AND WHEN Mrs. Roosevelt walked out, she went to a standing ovation. The sight of an honest woman, respectful of the right of her listeners to differ, but loyal also to her own beliefs, was a reminder of the strength and decency of the democratic tradition which shook all but the most doctrinaire.

It was a memorable occasion. And a few months later Mrs. Roosevelt's audience began to recollect it with a vivid comprehension.

War was no longer something to debate: war existed.

England evacuated Dunkirk in the spring of 1940, France fell and the writing was on the wall.

F.D.R.: December seventh, 1941 — a date which will live in infamy . . .

the United States of America was suddenly
and deliberately attacked by naval
and air forces of the empire of Japan . . .
Hostilities exist. There is no blinking at
the fact that our people, our territory and our
interests are in grave danger . . .

GUAM FELL on the thirteenth, Wake on
the twentieth.

The great British battleships, *Prince of Wales* and *Repulse,* were sunk by Japanese
aircraft off the Malay coast.

Hong Kong surrendered on Christmas Day.
Eight days later Manila fell and the
Americans in the Philippines were cut off on
the Bataan peninsula.

The British lost an army at Singapore and
naval units of Great Britain, the
Netherlands, and the United States were
beaten in the battle of the Java Sea.

Every news bulletin was a new disaster.

Six months after Pearl Harbor, the Nazis
were seventy miles from Alexandria in Egypt
and had taken Sevastopol on the Black Sea
and invested Stalingrad, while Britain, starved
by Nazi submarines and bombed by Nazi
planes, was quite literally fighting for its life.

To most Americans in those terrible months
the one task was the prosecution of the war,
the one end and aim the survival of the
country. But not to Eleanor Roosevelt.

Not even the greatest cataclysm in history
could quiet her conscience; what mattered to
her was not survival only but the *things* that
survived.

When she discovered that the Japanese-Americans of California and the coast had been herded into American concentration camps in the panic that followed Pearl Harbor, she protested. For one thing, the whole idea of the concentration camp was abhorrent to a free society. For another there was no proof — and history bore her out — that Japanese-Americans were less loyal than other Americans.

There could hardly have been a more unpopular cause in that place and time but she fought it out, and by fighting it, helped to fix her countrymen's attention on the real human cause — the cause of human decency and self-respect. This, throughout the war, was her continuing mission: to keep the human perspective.

She traveled the country from one end to the other to serve it.

In the fall of 1942 American troops in England were about to leave, though she didn't know it at the time, for the North African invasion. The President wanted her to visit the camps, so she flew the Atlantic in a commercial amphibian at her own expense; froze in cold austerity of Buckingham Palace; went from American camp to American camp; talked to British women . . .

MRS. ROOSEVELT: Thank you ladies and gentlemen. I am very grateful for the welcome which you have extended and very grateful for the opportunity to learn, which is my real reason for coming to this country. I apologize to all of you whom I have made stand in the rain this morning. I think it must have been a very disagreeable experience. But . . . having spent three years at school in England, I know that it's not an unusual one.

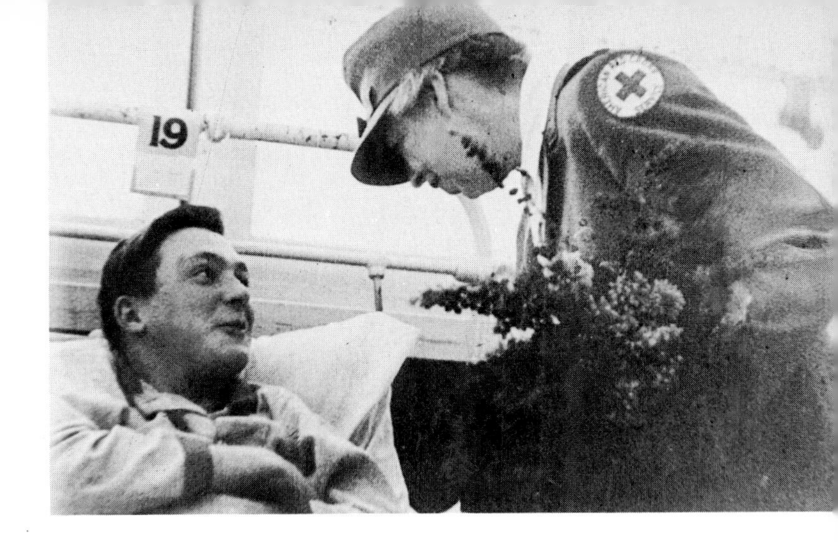

A YEAR LATER she crossed the Pacific; traveled 25,000 miles through seventeen Pacific islands; visited hospitals and bases; recreation centers and nurses homes; ate breakfast with enlisted men at unlikely hours; lost thirty pounds; talked to enormous audiences; and came home tireder than she had ever been in her life, to tell anyone who would listen of the *feel* of her experience — "the horrible consciousness of waste" which the hospitals left with her — to try to prepare the families of wounded boys for their return.

MRS. ROOSEVELT: The first thing is to write cheerful letters. The next thing, I believe, is to prepare yourselves for the return of your men. Some of them are coming back wounded, some of them are going to face handicaps all their lives, their feeling of confidence will depend on your being prepared to help them earn a living and enjoy life.

IT USED TO BE SAID at that time that Eleanor Roosevelt was her husband's eyes and ears, but it was never as simple as all that. For one thing she was her husband's wife and had to take the consequences. As she discovered in New Zealand when she told a story she had picked up in her travels.

MRS. ROOSEVELT: Just as the Marines were ordered to leave Guadalcanal, an officer found a private feeling very sad, looking very depressed. And he said, "What's the matter with you?" and he said, "Oh, I just can't go home — I haven't shot a Jap."

And so the officer said, "Well, listen, I'll tell you what to do. You go up to that ridge over there and jump up all of a sudden say 'To hell with Hirohito.' And there'll jump up other people all around you and if you shoot first you'll get a Jap."

And so he came by a little while later and the Marine was still looking very gloomy and he said, "Did you do what I told you to do?" and he said, "Yes, sir, yes, I ran up there and I did just what you told me to do and I said 'To hell with Hirohito.' And they jumped up just as you told me they would, but they all shouted 'To hell with Roosevelt.' "

TWENTY MONTHS later her husband died at Warm Springs in Georgia.

When the news came she flew south at once, returning in the train with the President's body. All through the April night she kept the window shade open beside her berth so that she could see the faces of the crowds in the dimly lighted stations and at the country crossroads . . .

She thought, she said, about the ballad of the lonely train that carried Lincoln's body to Springfield.

And when morning came and the caisson with its flag-covered coffin had come down between silent, weeping crowds from the Union Station in Washington to the White House, she was waiting.

She walked slowly down the steps beneath the portico and touched the flag.

And she was waiting too at the funeral in the East Room of the White House: it seemed to her, she said, that everyone in the world was there "except three of my own sons" — two of them sailors, one a soldier.

And afterwards as the great of the world came to leave their wreaths on the grave of the dead President, she was still waiting . . . looking forward . . . looking back . . .

She said, once, that Franklin Roosevelt "might have been happier with a wife who was completely uncritical."

But she said, too, "I think I sometimes acted as a spur, even though the spurring was not always wanted or welcome.

"I was one of those," she said, "who served his purposes."

But she was also one of those who gave his purposes their meaning and their words.

On the sixth of June in 1944, when the whole mind of the Republic was fixed on the beaches of Normandy, Eleanor Roosevelt had spoken to the women of her own country, and beyond them to the women of the world.

"Every woman," she said, "will be praying that the victory may be speedy and that, this time, the sacrifices, whatever they are, will bring results that will justify, in the eyes of those who fight, whatever they have gone through."

And then she added, "It is not enough to win the fight. We must win *that for which we fight* — the triumph of all people who believe that the people of this world are worthy of freedom."

One can see of course what she was remembering. Her mind had gone back twenty-five years. *"This time"* the victory must be worthy of the suffering that bought it. "This time" we must win not only the fight but that *for which* we fight.

"This time," we must remember our purposes, our cause, not only in the hour of anguish but in the hour of happiness when the troops return.

All this was in her mind when she looked back from her husband's death, a few months before the war had ended. But when she looked the other way, into the future, she saw nothing.

She didn't matter any more. What had mattered was the President and he was dead — his work finished — "the glory left behind him for the others."

To the reporters who met her in the train shed of the Pennsylvania Station when she returned to New York on her way to anonymity, she said, "The story is over."

But of course, the story wasn't over. In a sense it had just begun.

In the last fifteen years of her life, Eleanor Roosevelt, who had been the remarkable wife of a great President, became *herself* — became indeed, more than herself — became something very close to the conscience of her generation. And not in her own country alone but throughout the world: something very close to the voice of a common humanity which had had no voice before.

It all began when President Truman appointed her, eight months after her husband's death, to the American delegation to the first, the organizational, meeting of the General Assembly of the United Nations, to be convened in London in January of '46.

No one, including Eleanor Roosevelt, was enthusiastic about the appointment. She thought she was not qualified — an opinion the rest of the delegation, particularly the Republicans, Dulles and Vandenberg, warmly endorsed. Mr. Truman, however, insisted, and the event proved him right.

Assigned by her colleagues to Committee Three which was to deal with humanitarian and social and cultural matters and where, obviously, she could do the least harm, she soon found herself at the center of the hottest fight of the session — the fight over the Russian demand that all refugees be forced to return to their own countries regardless of what their countries had become in the interim — as, for example, Communist satellites.

Ultimately the debate reached the floor of the Assembly where Andrei Vishinsky, head of the Russian delegation and the most formidable advocate in the Assembly presented the Soviet case.

Who was to represent the United States?

Her fellow delegates, not eager themselves for the honor, appealed to their "unqualified" colleague.

MRS. ROOSEVELT: I gather that Mr. Vishinsky felt that anyone who did not wish to return under the present forms of government must of necessity be Fascist. I talked to a great many of these people: their country they feel no longer belongs to them. They did not strike me as Fascist.

AND ELEANOR ROOSEVELT scored a notable victory, carrying the Assembly with her against every one of the Soviet amendments.

It was a victory won without triumph without leaving bitterness behind. And by the end of the session it was obvious to everyone in London — including the members of the American delegation itself — that the most effective American in the General Assembly was Eleanor Roosevelt.

It was a *personal* effectiveness.

During the debates in the U.N. over Palestine and the Arab-Israeli war, she learned that her country's policy and the policy of the U.N. was under attack in the State Department and the Department of Defense, and she felt compelled to tell the President that if the agreed policy were altered she would have to express her feelings publicly — and would, of course, resign from the United States delegation before doing so . . .

The attacks ceased.

She was beginning to be treated, her critics complained, like a sovereign power — and sometimes they seemed to be right. Certainly the press of the world treated her correspondence with Cardinal Spellman of New York, on one famous occasion, as though it had been an exchange of State papers.

The Cardinal had taken exception to Mrs. Roosevelt's view on federal aid to parochial schools, and had published an open letter charging her with "discrimination unworthy of an American mother."

She replied in a personal letter assuring the Cardinal that she had "no sense of being 'an unworthy American mother.' The final judgment, my dear Cardinal Spellman, of the worthiness of all human beings is in the hands of God."

Her letter was published in full in the *Times* and eventually, after the Cardinal had called at Hyde Park for tea, a joint statement was issued asserting Mrs. Roosevelt's intention of continuing to say what she believed, and affirming the Cardinal's confidence in "the American right of free speech which not only permits but encourages differences of opinion."

Eleanor Roosevelt's greatest talent, as the world came more and more to see, was her ability to reduce the quarrels of doctrine and dogma to human differences which could be discussed in human terms.

MRS. ROOSEVELT: We must be able to disagree with people and to consider new ideas and not to be afraid . . .

THAT SHE HERSELF was not afraid was demonstrated in what has come to be called the McCarthy era, when the Junior Senator from Wisconsin had launched his inquisition into the opinions of his fellow citizens.

MRS. ROOSEVELT: The day that I am afraid to sit down in a room with people that I do not know because perhaps five years from now someone will say, "You sat in the room — five people were Communists — you are a Communist" — that will be a bad day. We must preserve our right to think and to differ in the United States."

"TO THINK and to differ," you could write a definition of America on that text — as well as the story of Eleanor Roosevelt's greatest achievement. It was because she believed — really believed — in the right of human beings to think and to differ that she became, toward the end of her life, a symbol of the American aspiration, and therefore of the belief in humanity for which the American aspiration had always stood.

And it was because the world thought of her in these terms that she became Chairman of the United Nations Commission appointed to draft a universal declaration of Human Rights. President Truman had named her as American representative on the Commission, but it was the members of the Commission themselves who elected her Chairman.

CHAIRMAN

MRS. ROOSEVELT: I don't know how other people feel but I always get a lift out of the fact that you can hear all the criticism and still have faith that the majority of the people will be right. I think it is always a very encouraging thing, and one which we in the Human Rights Commission must have tremendous faith in, because that's really the way that human rights will come to be a reality — only as the people really come to believe in human rights, and want to live for human rights.

IT WAS largely because of her chairmanship that the Commission was able, after two years of exhausting debate, to agree on a draft.

That draft was presented on December 10, 1948, to a meeting of the General Assembly under the presidency of Dr. Evatt of Australia.

DR. EVATT: We'll turn therefore to the first portion of this proclamation of universal declaration of human rights. We'll turn to the articles. We'll have to take them in turn.

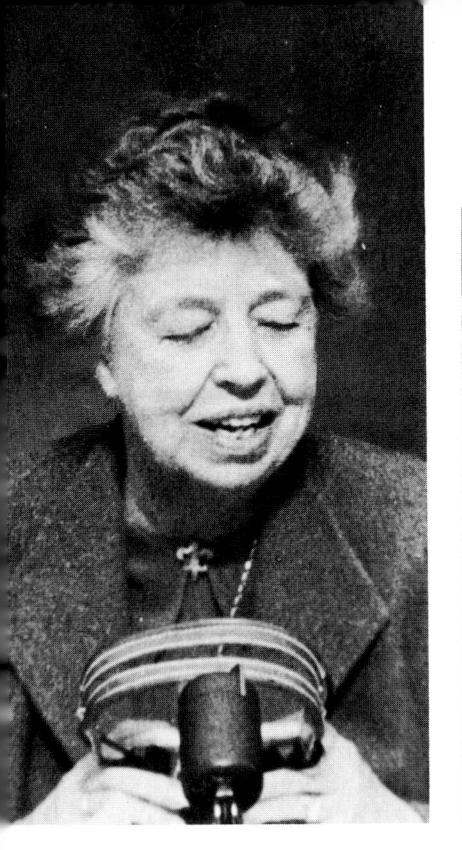

SSR
PHILIPPINES

DECLARACION UNIVERSAL
DE Derechos del Hombre
UNIDAS

Article One: All human beings are born free and equal in dignity and rights . . .

IT WAS three o'clock in the morning; the room was half empty as the voting went on, clause by clause, until at last the draft had been approved.

DR. EVATT: The General Assembly proclaims this declaration of human rights as a common standard of achievement for all people in all nations to the end that every individual and every organ of society shall strive by teaching and education to promote respect for these rights and freedoms . . .

So that we reach the stage, gentlemen, in which, by an enormous vote and without any direct opposition, this Assembly has adopted this very important Declaration. It is the first occasion on which the organized community of nations has made a declaration of human rights and fundamental freedoms, and it has the authority of the body of opinion of the U.N. as a whole. Millions of people, men, women and children all over the world many miles from Paris and New York, will turn for hope and guidance and inspiration to this document. It is particularly fitting that here tonight should be the person who has been the leader in this movement, assisted though she has been by many others — the person who has raised to even greater honor so great a name . . .

I refer, of course, to Mrs. Roosevelt, the delegate of the United States.

THE FIGURE that emerges in those last full years is a figure without likeness in our history. The lonely little girl in the dark parlor on Thirty-seventh Street who asked only to be left to her unhappiness had become a woman known by sight to millions of human beings and by repute to nearly all the world — a woman who stood for compassion and hope in every continent of the earth — for courage and for belief; a woman who met the great and the simple with the same simplicity giving and taking what she had given and taken all her life; the sense of humanity, of human worth.

She was still "plain" if that is, or ever was, the right word for her candid, selfless face, but no one who looked at her now ever thought of her plainness: only of her eyes. She was old: but it was her youth you saw when you met her.

She was a "great lady," as everyone kept saying over and over — "the first lady of the world" — but what the world found in her was a woman — a warm, completely honest, fearless woman who lived a woman's life, accepted a woman's responsibilities, and changed the history of her time.

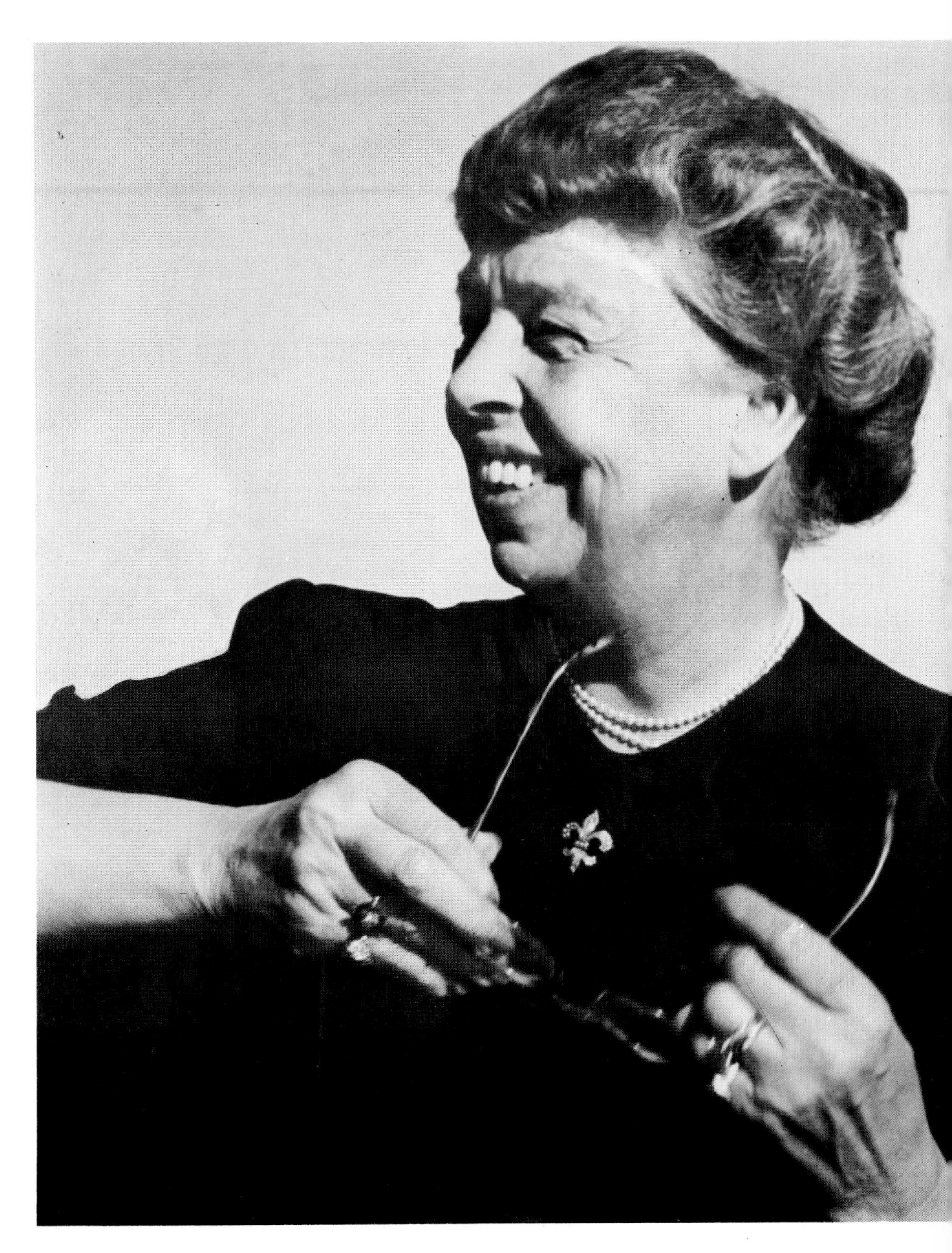

Grateful acknowledgment is made to Mr. Sidney Glazier, producer of the film *The Eleanor Roosevelt Story,* and to all members of his staff, for their generosity in making available the pictures that appear in this book. Appreciation is also extended to government bureaus, foreign agencies, and all others who have contributed materials and services toward the preparation of the book.

The picture of Mrs. Roosevelt on the front of the jacket and opposite page 1 appears by courtesy of the Eleanor Roosevelt Cancer Foundation.

Some of the pictures in this book were taken from newsreels supplied by the film libraries of the following organizations: John E. Allen, Inc., Hearst Metrotone News, Movietone News, Inc., Sherman Grinberg Film Libraries, Inc., the United Nations Film Library, and Universal Pictures, Inc. These pictures appear on the following pages: 28 (bottom), 33, 34, 36 (top and bottom), 37 (all pictures), 38 (top and bottom), 39, 46 (bottom), 48 (top), 49 (all pictures), 51, 52, 53, 54, 58, 61 (top and bottom), 63, 64, 65 (all pictures), 66 (top and bottom), 68, 70, 72, 74 (top), 75, 76, 77, 78 (top), 85 (top, bottom left), 86, 87, (top and bottom), 90, 95 (top — both pictures).

Many pictures were made available by the Franklin D. Roosevelt Library in Hyde Park, New York. These pictures appear on the following pages: 2, 3, 4, 5 (all pictures), 6 (top and bottom), 7 (the two pictures of the house at Tivoli), 8, 10 (bottom, a New York *Post* photograph), 14, 16 (all pictures except that of Mlle Souvestre with her pupils), 17 (all pictures), 18 (both pictures), 19 (both pictures), 20 (top and bottom), 21 (all pictures except those of Brown's Hotel, of Paris, and of London), 22 (top and bottom), 23 (all pictures), 24 (top and bottom), 25 (top and bottom), 26 (top), 27 (top and bottom), 35, 40, 41, 43 (top and bottom), 44 (top and bottom), 45, 46 (top), 47 (top and bottom), 48 (bottom), 50, 55, 57, 59, 62, 78 (bottom), 79, 81, 83, 84 (a New York *Times* photograph), 89, 91, 93, 95 (bottom, a UNATIONS photograph), 97, 99 (A. F. P. — a Jean Manzon photograph).

The picture of Mrs. Hall on page 7 was donated by Mrs. Morrison Colladay from her private collection. The picture of Allenswood School on page 15 and the picture of Mlle Souvestre with her pupils on page 16 were donated by Miss Helen Gifford from her private collection. The picture of Mrs. Roosevelt on page 32 was donated by James Roosevelt from his collection. The picture in the lower right corner of page 85 was donated by the Wiltwyck School for Boys.

The photographs on pages 9 and 11 (bottom) are by Percy C. Byron and are from the Byron Collection in the Museum of the City of New York. The photograph on page 13 is by Jacob A. Riis and is in the Riis Collection of the Museum of the City of New York.

The newspaper article reproduced in part on page 30 is from the Washington *Star* of June 22, 1919. The picture of Brown's Hotel on page 21 (second from top, at right) is used by courtesy of Trust Houses Ltd. The exterior view of St. Elizabeth's Hospital on page 29 appears by courtesy of that hospital. The other pictures on page 29 are used by courtesy of the National Association for Mental Health; the picture at the lower left is a photograph by Lord. The pictures on page 28 (top) and 31 (both pictures) are reproduced by permission of the American Red Cross. The pictures on pages 74 (bottom) and 80 (bottom) are U.S. Coast Guard photographs, and the picture on page 80 (top) is a U.S. Army photograph. The picture on page 82 is used by courtesy of the National Foundation. The pictures on pages 10 (top), 11 (top), 12 (top and bottom), 21 (the pictures of London and of Paris) are from the Library of Congress.

This book was designed by Robert L. Barry.